NINA LEARNS ABOUT SERVICE ANIMALS

The Nina Learns Series 1

Hannah Goodbody

Nina Learns About Service Animals
Copyright © 2024 by Hannah Goodbody

All rights reserved. No part of this publication may be reproduced, distributed, or transmitted in any form or by any means, including photocopying, recording, or other electronic or mechanical methods, without the prior written permission of the author, except in the case of brief quotations embodied in critical reviews and certain other non-commercial uses permitted by copyright law.

Tellwell Talent
www.tellwell.ca

ISBN
978-0-2288-9439-1 (Hardcover)
978-0-2288-9438-4 (Paperback)

DEDICATION

I would like to dedicate this story to my husband and daughter, who are the inspiration for this story. I would also like to thank my family and friends for their support as I completed this book during a very busy time in my life. Without them, I would have never been able to finish it.

WHAT INSPIRED THE SERIES

The inspiration for this series is my beautiful daughter. Nina reflects my daughter and her insatiable curiosity for the world around her. *Nina Learns About Service Animals* is a story inspired by a true event. On that day, many people were trying to pat the guide dog, unknowingly making it harder for the guide dog to do his job. I wanted to make sure there was another book out there to help kids and their parents learn how to interact with (or not interact with) service animals.

KIKI:
Nina, would you like to go for a walk in the park?

NINA:
YAY! I'll go grab Foxy!

NINA:
Yay! We're finally here, Mama! I'm so excited! Can we feed the birds sunflower seeds and the squirrels some peanuts? I have some in Foxy next to my water bottle!

KIKI:
Absolutely, my love! Sunflower seeds and peanuts are both safe foods for birds and squirrels.

NINA:
There are so many people walking dogs! Can I pet some dogs, Mama?

KIKI:
Only if their owners say it's okay. Introduce yourself to the dogs the way I taught you, putting your hand down low and letting them sniff you first.

KIKI:
Let's try not to scare them away.

NĪNA:
Oh, Mama, can I go pet that dog please?

KIKI:
No, sweetie. I'm sorry, but we can't pet that dog. That's a working dog, so we can't play with or distract this dog.

ÑINA:
Mama, what's a working dog?

KIKI:
A working dog is a dog with an important job. That dog we saw is a guide dog. Sometimes guide dogs are called seeing-eye dogs. Guide dogs help people who have trouble seeing to get around safely.

NINA:
Mama, are working dogs like my glasses?
Do working dogs help people see?

KIKI:
Sort of. Guide dogs help people who can't see very well to get around the world more safely. For example, we know when it's safe to cross the road because we can see the walking person telling us when it's safe to go, but some people can't see the walking person, so it's their dog's job to help them know when it is safe to cross. Guide dogs help their owners by making sure that they don't bump into anything or get lost. For people with trouble seeing, a guide dog is like having a best friend who always knows the way and helps keep you safe when walking.

ÑINA:
But Mama, dogs can't talk, so how do they let their owners know when it is safe to cross?

KIKI:
Guide dogs are amazing helpers! They can keep their owners safe by pulling and guiding their owners around obstacles and even telling them when to stop. For example, if there's a dangerous place like a road, the guide dog might step in front of their owner to block the way, telling them to stop and keep their owner from getting hurt. Together, the person and their guide dog will decide when it's safe to cross the street and how to get around safely. Sometimes, the dog will gently pull their owner forward when it's time to cross, while the owner will always listen carefully to make sure they're safe.

ÑINA:
Then, I can't pet the dog because he's helping that man right now.

KIKI:
Exactly! We don't want to distract the dog from their important job of helping to keep their owner safe.

NINA:
Are there a lot of dogs with important jobs? Dog jobs, that sounds fun to say!

KIKI:
Yes, there are a lot of different jobs that working animals or service animals can have, such as hearing dogs, who help people like me who can't hear very well, they let the person know when a doorbell or a fire alarm is ringing. There are dogs who help the police to find missing people, or they might smell for things like food and objects, like at the airport. Some dogs will let people know when they're about to have a medical emergency like a seizure, a diabetic sugar drop, or another medical event. There are hundreds of different jobs that service dogs or other animals can have.

NINA:
What other types of animals can be service animals?

KIKI:
Well, service animals can be any animal, but more commonly they are dogs, cats, miniature or full-sized horses, and birds. A service animal is any animal that has been specifically trained and certified to help their human companions live more independent, safe, and happy lives.

KIKI:
Whatever the service animal might be doing, it's important not to interrupt or distract them from their job.

NINA:
Do service animals ever get to relax and play?

KIKI:
Yes, they can! Just like people, service animals need to take breaks and rest too. When they're not working, they get to do fun things like play, eat, and sleep. But they must be ready to help their owners when they need them. So, it's important to not bother them, especially when they are wearing their special vests, because that means that they're busy working. Remember, you can always ask questions to learn more about service animals and you can also go online and look up information if you aren't sure.

NĪNA:
Thanks, Mama! I hope one day, I get to learn how to be a service animal trainer!

KIKI:
That would be a fantastic and very important job!

THE END

Printed in the USA
CPSIA information can be obtained
at www.ICGtesting.com
JSHW041907081124
73202JS00002B/12